HORSES

SHETLAND PONIES

JANET L. GAMMIE

ABDO & Daughters

Published by Abdo & Daughters, 4940 Viking Drive, Suite 622, Edina, Minnesota 55435.

Library bound edition distributed by Rockbottom Books, Pentagon Tower, P.O. Box 36036, Minneapolis, Minnesota 55435.

Printed in the United States.

Cover Photo credit: Peter Arnold, Inc.

Interior Photo credits: Peter Arnold, Inc.

Edited by Bob Italia

Library of Congress Cataloging-in-Publication Data

Gammie, Janet L.
    Shetland Ponies/ Janet L. Gammie.
        p.   cm. — (Horses)
Includes bibliographical references (p.23) and index.
    ISBN 1-56239-438-X
1. Shetland pony—Juvenile literature. [1. Shetland pony. 2. Ponies.] I. Title.
II. Series Gammie, Janet L. Horses.
SF315.2.S5G36   1995
636.1'6—dc20   95-2237
                                                          CIP
                                                          AC

ABOUT THE AUTHOR
    Janet Gammie has worked with thoroughbred race horses for over 10 years. She trained and galloped thoroughbred race horses while working on the racetracks and farms in Louisiana and Arkansas. She is a graduate of Louisiana Tech University's Animal Science program with an equine specialty.

Contents

WHERE SHETLANDS CAME FROM

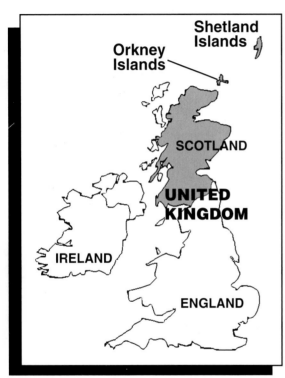

Horses are mammals just like humans. Mammals are **warm-blooded** animals with a backbone. The horse's earliest **ancestor** was *Eohippus* (e-oh-HIP-us). It lived about 50 million years ago.

The Shetland is one of the oldest pony **breeds**. It comes from Scotland's Orkney and Shetland islands.

The Shetland developed into a work horse. The Scotsmen used the pony to haul **peat** for their fires. Later the Shetland hauled coal in mines. In time, children rode these small hardy ponies.

The Shetland is one of the ancient pony breeds. It came from Scotland's Orkney and Shetland islands.

The Scottish Shetland and the American Shetland look very different. The Scottish Shetland looks like a tiny draft horse. Draft horses are large and strong. They are used for pulling heavy loads. The American Shetland is more graceful and refined. Today they are used as cart ponies and children's riding ponies.

WHAT SHETLANDS LOOK LIKE

The American Shetland has large eyes and a fine jaw with short erect ears. It has a small **muzzle** and large nostrils. The Shetland has a strong body and big muscles. Its **mane** and tail are long and thick. This gives warmth in very cold weather.

The largest Shetlands are 46 inches (117 cm) or 11 hands high (hh). Each hand equals 4 inches (10 centimeters). They can weigh 400 to 600 pounds (181 to 272 kilograms).

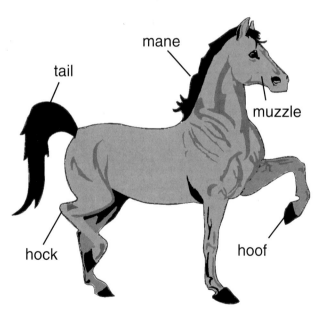

Horses share the same features.

**The Shetland has a strong body. Its mane and tail
are long and thick.**

Most Shetlands are stubborn and strong-willed
toward adult humans. Around children they are usually
more gentle.

WHAT MAKES SHETLANDS SPECIAL

Shetland ponies are **bred** for their strength and size. They can pull up to 1,200 pounds (544 kilograms)—three times their body weight. Because of their strength they make good cart ponies for adults. However, their backs are not strong enough to carry an adult rider for very long.

On the Orkney and Shetland islands, food was hard to find. Sometimes the ponies ate seaweed to survive. The Shetland's pulling and survival skills makes it a strong pony.

Although the Shetland is a strong horse, its back can only support an adult rider for a short time.

COLOR

Shetlands can be bay, chestnut, black, roan, gray, albino and pinto. Bay can be light or dark brown bodies with black points. Points are the leg, **mane** and tail.

A horse with brown hair and the same color or lighter points is a chestnut. Black horses have all black hairs and can have white **markings**. Roan is one basic color with one or more colors added. Gray horses have white and black hairs on black skin.

Pinto is white with any uneven, colored spots. Albinos have pink skin, eyes and white hair. Albino animals do not have the **pigment** it takes to make color. Silver and gold dapples are the most popular colors. Dapples are darker spots of the same color.

Shetland markings are solid white patches on the head and legs. Head markings are star, stripe, blaze, snip, and bald face. Leg markings are ankle, sock and stocking. Shetlands can have any mix of head or leg markings.

Shetlands can have solid white patches on their body, head and legs.

STAR   **STRIPE**   **SNIP**   **BLAZE**   **BALD FACE**

CARE

Vaccinations are given to the pony to help prevent disease. Sometimes ponies get sick or hurt even with the best of care. When this happens it is best to call the veterinarian. A veterinarian is an animal doctor. They care for animals just like doctors care for people.

Regular **deworming** helps prevent parasites inside the horse's body. A parasite is a bug that lives off another animal. Ponies' teeth are floated, or filed down, once a year after they are two years old. This keeps the teeth even and lets the horse chew correctly.

There are many different brush types to **groom** the pony. Soft brushes are used on the face and legs. Stiffer brushes are used on the rest of the body. Always clean around the eyes and nose with a soft towel. **Hoof** picks are made for cleaning the small places in the hoof.

Because of their thick mane, Shetlands need brushing often.

FEEDING

Ponies out to **pasture** do not need more food unless they are working or are **pregnant**. It is important to remove all harmful plants from a pasture. A pasture should also be free of harmful things such as wire and nails. If a pony is hungry it may eat poisonous or harmful plants. Some poisonous plants are nightshade, thistle and horse nettle.

Soil and climate decide the grass types planted in a pasture. Bluegrass and bromegrass are often grown. A pony out to pasture eats grass filled with **minerals** important for good health. Minerals should be fed to the pony if it is kept in a **stall**.

Shetlands out to pasture eat grass which is filled with minerals important for good health.

THINGS SHETLANDS NEED

How a pony is used will decide what **tack** it will need. If the Shetland is a cart pony then it will wear a **harness**. A harness wraps around the pony's body. It will allow the horse to use its entire body to pull the cart. If the pony is used for riding, then a **saddle** and **bridle** are needed.

All tack should fit properly for the pony's comfort. Bad-fitting tack may cause sores and bad habits. This will make the ride unhappy for the pony and rider.

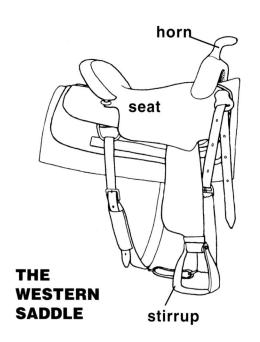

horn

seat

THE WESTERN SADDLE

stirrup

How a pony is used will decide what tack it will need. A saddle and bridle are used for riding.

HOW SHETLANDS GROW

A baby horse is called a foal. A foal lives inside the **mare's** body for about 11 months. The mare will lick the foal clean when it is born.

As she cleans the foal she will nicker to the baby. Nickering is one of the noises that horses and ponies make. The mare also nickers to the foal as it tries to stand. The foal should stand within 15 minutes of birth.

After the foal is standing, the mare gently nudges and nickers to her foal so it will **nurse**.

The first milk has colostrum in it. Colostrum is thick and full of antibodies. An antibody is a **protein** that is found in the blood. These antibodies protect the foal from harmful diseases.

The mare will nurse the foal 15 minutes after birth.
The antibodies found in the mare's milk will protect
the foal from diseases.

TRAINING

Training begins early in the foal's life. The foal learns to wear a **halter** a few days after birth. Ponies are handled easily at an early age. Because they are young, they accept people and are less likely to hurt someone. A pony's natural response is to run from danger. Until they learn to trust people, they will try to get away by running or kicking.

Always approach a foal quietly and slowly. In time, the foal will trust people and will let a person approach. Soon the foal will learn to lead or walk on a rope beside a person.

Ponies should be handled with care at an early age. Then they will learn to trust people.

GLOSSARY

ANCESTOR (AN-ses-tor) - An animal from which other animals are descended.

BREED - A kind or type; also to produce young.

BRIDLE - The part of the harness that fits over the horse's head (including the bit and reins), used to guide or control the animal.

DEWORMING (de-WURM-ing) - To take away worms.

GROOM - To clean.

HALTER - A rope or strap for leading or tying an animal.

HARNESS - The leather straps, bands, and other pieces used to hitch a horse to a carriage, wagon, or plow.

HOOF - A horse's foot.

MANE - The long, heavy hair on the back of a horse's neck.

MARE - The female of certain animals, such as horse, donkey, or zebra.

MARKINGS - The white color on the head and legs.

MINERAL (MIN-er-el) - A substance obtained by mining or digging in the earth.

MUZZLE - The part of an animal's head that extends forward and contains the nose, mouth, and jaws.

NURSE - To feed a foal from the mother's breast.

PASTURE - A grassy field or hillside.

PEAT - Partly rotted moss and plants, used as fuel after being dried.

PIGMENT - A substance, such as chlorophyll, that gives color to plant or animal tissues.

PREGNANT - Carrying a baby inside the body.

PROTEIN - A substance containing nitrogen which is a necessary part of plant and animal cells.

SADDLE - A seat for a rider on a horse's back.

STALL - A place where a horse is housed.

TACK - Equipment horses use.

VACCINATE (VAK-si-nate) - To give a shot.

WARM-BLOODED - Having blood that stays the same temperature, even though the surroundings change. Birds and mammals are warm-blooded animals.

BIBLIOGRAPHY

Casey, Brigid and Lavin, Sigmund A. *Wonders of Ponies.* Dodd, Mead and Company, New York, 1980.

Millar, Jane. *Birth of a Foal.* J.B. Lippincott Company, New York, 1977.

Petty, Kate. *Ponies and Foals.* Gloucester Press, New York, 1990.

Possell, Elsa. *Horses.* Childrens Press, Chicago, 1961.

Index